About the Author

Laura, also known as 'The Happiness Coach', considers it her mission in life to help uplift the planet and encourage a shift in the consciousness that people have today. Laura currently does one to one coaching through her website to help others achieve their goals, fulfill their dreams and awaken their connection to the Universe.

EMBRACING YOUR DIVINITY

Laura Emily

EMBRACING YOUR DIVINITY

Vanguard Press

VANGUARD PAPERBACK

© Copyright 2018
Laura Emily

A CIP catalogue record for this title is
available from the British Library.

ISBN 978 1 784654 08 5

Vanguard Press is an imprint of
Pegasus Elliot MacKenzie Publishers Ltd.
www.pegasuspublishers.com

First Published in 2018

Vanguard Press
Sheraton House Castle Park
Cambridge England

Printed & Bound in Great Britain

Dedication

This book is dedicated to Mr Robert Martin, a true gentleman, the spark in my life, and the man who introduced me to my true self.

Acknowledgments

I am eternally grateful to all the individuals who took part in my journey and will continue to take the wisdom that they have taught me and use it in my own life now, as I hope everyone who reads this book does.

To Bobby, who turned my life around the moment we spoke, who brought out the best in me and continues to do so now. The man who makes me laugh like no other, who I trust eternally and who I am blessed to share my life with, I love you.

To my Mum, who has been there through everything and has shown me what unconditional love is. She is the woman who taught me to be wise and taught me that love is always worth reaching for.

To my Dad, who showed me what true ambition is. He taught me to never give up, to always keep trying and that life is not as tough as it always appears to be. I truly get my care free ways from this man.

To my sisters, who make being a big sister the most fun job ever. I always receive great value in their ways and they always make me see things I never saw before.

To my brother, who taught me to always take risk. He

taught me to chase my dreams but to be smart along the way. He was the first person I worked with and his strong worth ethics are still with me today.

And finally, a huge thank you to Stephen Conner for forwarding this book and to his wife, Dianne, who edited it and encouraged my work.

Go to bed, count your blessings, take them in your stride, put them under your belt and then get up tomorrow and do it all over again.

— My Grandad

Forward

There is a truth that lies within us all. In the guise of ancient wisdom, the way to this truth has been presented to us many times throughout the centuries. Due to the compulsive human need to control and own, this wisdom is often misplaced or misunderstood, or even abused as a foundation for misguided beliefs and ideologies. It is important therefore, for us all to gain an understanding of such wisdom. This wisdom is contained in universal laws and it is these laws that govern us all. With an understanding of these laws we can define our purpose, and give meaning to our very existence, and in turn help ourselves to find that ever eluding inner peace.

In this insightful book, Laura Emily shares her own unique perception of these laws, including the Law of Attraction. Her style is very personable, clear and has an innocence that exudes authenticity. These qualities are an example of the many benefits of directing your life to align with universal laws.

On Laura's journey, she gained inspiration from other awakened souls, people that have found their own truth. She beautifully blends their perspectives into the weaves of wisdom contained in her story. With an ever increasing need for each of us all to discover our own truth and uniqueness, *Embracing Your Divinity* will help guide you on your way.

In a world of extremes where harmony seems like an impossibility, it is almost essential that we all awaken our soul to find the real and authentic person that will help bring change and peace into the world. World peace begins with inner peace, they are inseparable. It has never been the responsibility of leaders or governments to bring peace, it has always been the responsibility of the individual to live a life that reflects the essence of peace and being *A Good Soul.*

This book will help to awaken your soul. As Laura takes you on her journey, as well as those that she has met on the way, you will be inspired with every turn of a page.

Preface

I have experienced a great journey of leaving my Ego behind and allowing the right side of my brain to take over and see the world around me for what it really is; and what it really is not what many believe or have been brought up to believe. Perhaps the reason you have picked up this book is because you already know that. My journey began when I discovered the *Law of Attraction* and so naturally, this is the part of my journey I want to share with you first.

This story is the tree trunk to my enlightenment. Starting with my own journey, I have branched out and been blessed by receiving the time and wisdom of many *good souls* who wish to also share their stories with you. These souls are not just any souls, they are my friends, relatives, inspiration and masters of these teachings. Some are all four, and I have been lucky enough to meet them along my precious journey.

Some have discovered the Law of Attraction and turned their lives around, some have had the pleasure of finding happiness and enjoying alignment, some have experienced physical manifestations, some have healed themselves and others are simply living in amazement every day as to what they can achieve. I hope that you can relate to our journeys and that they give you comfort in your *awakening.*

Introduction

To understand ones self, one must understand the infinite power that surrounds our mind, body and spirit. There are many universal laws that surround us, the Law of Attraction being one of them. It is the most powerful law within our Universe and it tells us that like energy attracts like energy. Our Universe shall always match the frequency in which our energy is vibrating. When we know this we notice it. When we look around, we see it. Those who are speaking of their lack are always losing out. Those who are speaking of their prosperity are always receiving.

We may all look like unique beings on the outside, but we are all the same within. We are all souls, here to create in this physical realm, but that soul, our inner being, is still with us. It is always with us, it just gets ignored sometimes.

We may look like we group together in friendship circles based on our similar interests and hobbies, but we do not. We are grouped together because our energy matches those around us. We may see a group of people sat around a table, laughing and giggling, and we may even notice that they all enjoy similar material things like clothes, jewellery and make-up, but actually underneath all that they are vibrating at the same frequency, which therefore draws them together. This is what is happening everywhere. It happens on a small and large scale.

The power that we have as a human race is phenomenal. We create everything as an individual and as a whole. We create the good and the not-so-good. We create the welcoming manifestations and the detrimental ones. We create the physical wealth and the physical disease. We create the emotional abundance and the emotional turmoil. We create the sunshine and we create the hurricanes.

We are always being guided. When we walk into a situation where the energy does not feel good we naturally walk away. This is not because it does not match ours, because it does; it is because we have experienced a sense of our own negative energy and left it behind. It is like walking into a physical manifestation of your own negativity and you did not like it. If we did not like it when we walked into the room then why would we hold it in our hearts? We feel it in different ways, through different urges and cravings, we walk this way, go that way, talk to this person, avoid that person. It all seems like every day life, but what is truly happening is that you are a magnet. My soulful friend Stephen Conner, author of *'The Divine Spirit'* and who also appears in this book, calls it your 'inner magnet', which is extremely accurate. That magnet attracts only to its counterpart and so we are naturally weaving in and out of different energies and frequencies depending on what frequency we are on. Therefore, happiness attracts happiness and sadness attracts sadness without fail. Our energy is always changing too. We tend to bob up and down on this universal current. Sometimes we stay aligned to it for a while, whilst other times we seem to dip in and out of it. This is why some days can feel like we are neither here nor there.

We also see this in the people we run into. We run into friends who make us laugh, we cross paths with those who are helpful, we float by the ones who are smiling. This is when we know we are vibrating at a high frequency. It is when we run into people that displease us, we cross paths with those who are impatient, we float by the ones who are frowning: that is when we know that we need to check back in with ourselves and connect with our inner being once again. The Universe is always right. The sooner we know this the sooner we can use it to our benefit and create abundantly, for we are abundant beings. We can use what is around us to see where we are at and fine tune our vibration to our benefit, or we can ignore it and act like it is wrong and believe that we cannot possibly be feeling that way and continue to struggle through everyday life as we always have. The choice is absolutely ours, but it is important to remind ourselves that the Universe is our friend and it is not showing us things to upset us, offend us, or create something purposely unpleasant. It is only ever matching us up to where we are at that moment in time. There is good in everything; if we know how to look for it. The Universe is never wrong. It never sends people to you to test you, only to teach you. If you are facing someone who is upsetting you then this is your indicator to pick yourself up.

The Universe is always guiding us to the best thought. It is always wanting us to be as aligned with it whenever possible. Every single moment in our lives we are learning something. Even if it is small, or seems small, there is something. We are constantly growing and expanding; there is evidence of it everywhere we look: if we look for it. The more we connect to our inner being the more we see things as the Universe does and so the more we see our power, our worth and our growth.

The Law of Attraction is always at play and we can never shut it down, it will never stop. Whether we can understand it or not; it will continue to be and so I ask you to ponder over its power and use it for its purpose. It is there for us to create a delicious experience.

Where my journey began

I started visualising when I was a child but I did not know how powerful my mind was at the time. I remember being around six years old and I was perhaps the only child around who loved going to bed. I never complained when it got to that time of the day (although my parents may disagree), because it was my time to visualise. I had begun to use my imagination a lot and so I loved my bedtime because it was my time to do exactly this. It would be the time where the house went quiet, the village went quiet and so did my mind. I remember imagining I had a merry-go-round in my garden and I would play and dance on it all night long. After a few weeks, my imagination expanded until I had an entire fair in my front garden and every night I would get excited to go to bed and play on it. This is my first memory of living within my own mind.

I was as young as nineteen when I had my first nudge from the Universe. I was walking our family dog across the blossomed forest with my mum when she told me about a book she was reading, *Ask and it's Given* by Esther and Jerry Hicks. This book is my go-to book now, but at the time I did not quite feel its power. These teachings had come to her attention when a rather lovely man swept into her life for a fleeting moment. He had discovered this book when his surroundings became nothing but a rented room and a shrivelled up twenty-pound note in his back pocket. After coming across this book through a friend he began applying these principles that were being shown to him and his life rapidly changed around him. A few years on from his journey my mum now had this rather lovely man sat in front of her telling her, 'You must buy this book', and buy the book she did... *eventually.*

After trying to apply the principles to her own life she decided to share them with me and I am so grateful that she did. I was young and at first I found it overwhelming to read. The content was different from anything I had ever read so I took the basic knowledge from it and did my best at the time to try and manifest something of my very own. This lasted a whole six days. I manifested little things like reasonably priced gym memberships, kind people and an extra fifteen pounds to my weekly wages, but slowly life got in the way and I got swept up in 'reality' once again. Little did I know that this was the start of something big.

1
The Universe

We are supposed to enjoy life, it is supposed to be fun and the Universe is always guiding us to that moment of exhilaration, if only we could all just allow it to. The Universe knows its own design and therefore it knows that in order for us to experience that instant manifestation we need to first be in alignment with our true selves. Our inner being can manifest with great ease as it bobs up and down on the universal currents, but it is us in these bodies and of these minds that disallow that to happen by overthinking and pushing something to move before it is ready. Not just before it is ready, before *we* are ready.

When we align with our inner being we create life which we know shall always be enjoyable. Alignment, in its most basic description is when we think, feel and play as our inner being does. We cannot force things into creation and when we are aligned we would not want to anyway. When we are aligned and when we are our true selves we see the Universe exactly as it is. We see that there are no mistakes, there are only pathways to remembering more about who we are. We know that there is no time, only moments built up amongst themselves to create our life experience.

When we are aligned we know that the Universe is bringing us things that we are already aligned to and we enjoy them in all of their beauty. We enjoy them so much that we do not think about the other things that have yet to arrive, they are irrelevant and they are not in the *now* moment. We know that the only reason they are not ready to be with us is because we are not ready to receive them: we have yet to align with them. We have to be a vibrational match to those desires before they can reach us. The Universe is built up of vibrations, this is the *Law of Vibration.* The *Law of Vibration* tells us that nothing in the Universe ever rests, it moves at a fast pace and if we align to those vibrations we draw them in. In order to do this we must be ready because God never gives us more than we can handle.

This does not mean that we will never be ready, in fact, we are already on our way to being ready because once we have asked for it, we are prepared to receive it. Nothing is received by chance, everything is received because we brought it to us using our thoughts, words and actions. This is the *Law of Cause and Effect.*

The Universe is sending us different types of people and circumstances that are allowing us to grow and create new thoughts and ideas, which are leading us to those things that not only do we think we want, but also to the person we think we really are, for we cannot create greatness without first finding it within ourselves.

We must always allow things to flow in and out of our experience. When we demand something we are not appreciating all the golden steps that we are taking, therefore it cannot come to us. It means that instead of going with the current we are pushing against it and this can be exhausting. It is not until we let go that things can start to happen. How many times have you been pushing for something until you are so exhausted you give up? It is then, at that moment, it arrives for us. This is the moment we start working with the Universe rather than against it. You see this all the time in couples who wish to be parents but are told they cannot. Have you ever heard of couples who adopt and then get pregnant right away? This is because they have stopped pushing against the Universal current and are enjoying parenthood so much it enabled their desire to conceive finally reach them in their alignment.

The Universe is on our side. It is us that is not always playing the game so to speak. The Universe never gets it wrong. If we have not received something that we think we want it is because we have not yet made a vibrational match to it, so it is important to realise that the Universe does know what you know, it wants you to be aligned with your desires, therefore it is doing all it can to get you there without fail. It may not seem like it, it may seem like you are struggling or you are confused about what to do next but it is always there. Perspective is everything. The more we understand that the Universe is doing its part to get us where we want to be, the more we can enjoy the adventure that it is taking us on. The Universe is never wrong and if it feels like something is off it is because we are off. We are not aligning with our inner being. We are always changing and growing and it is up to us to keep up with that which we are becoming because that which we are becoming is someone that knows, as the Universe knows, that everything is perfect just the way it is.

We are all creators. You are a creator and I am a creator. We are beautiful. I am beautiful, and you are beautiful. That feeling in our gut, our basic instincts, that voice is God gently guiding us to happiness. Happiness is our natural state of being. When we are happy we are at the top of our game and it is where our levels of consciousness lay. When we stay with it we can see as it sees, do as it does, and most importantly we love as it loves.

God loves everybody and every situation. The Universe sees the good in everything and the potential. It sees every circumstance as a blessing and sees it as a lesson, but unless we connect to it we do not see it. When we do align with it we can start to enjoy life as we should. Life is supposed to be fun. It is not supposed to always be a struggle or constant hard work. The more we struggle the more we are disconnected from God and our divinity. It can feel lonely there and makes us feel lost. God is our friend, one with us, and if we always stay connected to it then we are in for a wondrous life experience.

The Journey of Allison Phillips

I discovered the Law of Attraction about ten years ago when I was hooked up with a business mentor. He talked a lot about the Law of Attraction and the power of manifestation. This was my first exposure to it. I found it interesting but it did not grab my full attention at first until I started seeing a pattern to it. Every business coach I have had since him has talked about the Law of Attraction or mentioned it in some way. They would talk about the inner being, talk a lot about energy, focus and how important it was for our mindset to be in the right place. The more they talked about it the more I grew attracted to the teachings.

I never came at it from the point of view of trying to manifest something materialistic. It came to me more from an area of controlling my mindset and making sure I was aware of my thoughts and emotions. I wanted to know more and learn more: I was so curious. My entire experience of the Law of Attraction did not come to me through wanting a specific goal. My life was going fine, I did not need to manifest anything so I was more playful. For me, it was my relationships and changing the situations in my life. Manifesting confidence was my main aim as I often second-guessed myself. So for me, it was more of a desire to experience confidence inside myself and wanting to know I was manifesting and creating my own life experience. I had a deep desire to understand how it all worked. To me, the Law of Attraction was always secondary because I was focusing my attention more on myself. It was more about my mindset.

It was when I had my spiritual awakening in 2013 that I had a deeper awareness of it, but I never thought of it as visualising something specific; for me it was a realisation that this was how the world works. I became aware of my inner being and that we are vibrational beings living in a vibrational Universe. This totally opened up my mindset.

After this, it was about learning how to live my life on the highest frequency I could. The first manifestation for me was joy and nothing was going to take me away from this state of joy and clarity. The joy came first and then the manifestation came second. Once I found this, life around me became easier and from a business perspective, I did not have to hustle for clients, they just came to me. Everything started to flow into my experience.

I did not need to sit down and visualise; it went from a lot of hustle to a lot of ease—tremendous ease. It came from my alignment of source and who I truly was and even my relationships with others became easy too. They all flowed. Life felt so much easier to me. The more I understood who my being was, the more I was aware of my ability to manifest things in my life.

My mornings are very important to me and I use them to get myself ready for a great day. I always follow my bliss. I follow my joy and what I am most passionate about in that moment. Some days I wake up and I do not look at my phone. Instead, I just sit with great appreciation. I just want to be still and quiet. I feel the abundance of that. Other times I want to step out and walk in the park to be around nature. I see people scurrying around to get to work and I am just totally chilled. I see such a contrast between me and them. Sometimes I get up and want to work out first. Other times I want to enjoy a meditation. Sometimes I do it for fifteen minutes and other times for forty-five. I am not rigid about my meditation, I just want to enjoy it for what it is. Most days I want to meditate first because I love that feeling of leaving everything and going somewhere else, but after that I just follow my bliss. Sometimes I want to just go back to bed and take a nap which is interesting because I will get up at five, meditate, go for a walk and then come back and go straight to bed because ideas come to me as I am drifting off. They come to be because I am following my inner guidance. Sometimes naps inspire me, sometimes walks in nature inspire me and other times I get inspired by sitting on my deck and watching the sky. I want to always be open to what is the best way for me to receive my guidance and it shifts as I grow and how I feel that day. I love my time in the morning to continue to stay in that state of being.

For some people, they do things in the morning like meditate or go for a walk, but then get themselves caught up in a bad day and cannot understand why. We all have bad days but the reason we start out having a good one is not just to give us a head start, it is so we can carry that embodiment with us throughout the day. We can go back to that moment and enjoy it. I have a history of cultivating high flying emotions that I can reach for. I can go back to how I felt that morning and pluck out that feeling.

There are different levels of how you wake up. If you are feeling despair then you can try to reach for a happy thought, but it may be by doing that you are just irritating yourself more. You have to know where you are first. If I know I am having thoughts that are spiralling down and I try to reach for a better one I know it will not work because I am not a vibrational match to that thought. Sometimes you just have to accept that the day will just be what the day is! This can improve over time. I feel like I am in a pretty good habit of bouncing back to my alignment but I realise that although it has gotten easier over the years, sometimes we have to fall off because falling off is why we are here. Our souls were not brought here to prance around and be happy all the time, there is so much relevance in spiralling downwards. When I am not in a good mood I do not over analyse, I just own it and accept it. I do not let it discourage me. I like to look at it more as an observer.

You cannot have a thought without an emotion. You can think to yourself that you are in a bad mood, but that in itself is just a thought. It will not stick around so you do not need to think about it. What is a better thought? I am alive to live another day and I am about to go to the kitchen where I will have food and a coffee. You can switch quickly and learn to do this. You can also grab great memories. I am blessed to work from home so I can go sit out on my deck and gaze at the sky: I can enjoy the feeling of nature and feel the breeze. If I have a moment where I feel myself spiralling then I can just go back to that moment and feel the energy from it and re-live it. I create these types of moments purposely for myself every day. You do not need to make negative emotions a big deal. If

I fall, I am never too far from feeling better because I can always reach for it.

The greatest misunderstanding about manifestation is that we never stop manifesting. People ask me to teach them how to manifest but I tell them that we never stop manifesting, we are always manifesting, good or bad. There is never a time you are not manifesting. If you drive to work and have a great experience, you manifested that. If you drive to work and have a horrible experience, you manifested that. Human beings tend to have the ability to look at the manifestations outside themselves but do not always look at the manifestations within themselves. We wake up every day to manifest, we never stop, so the best thing to do is to wake up and fine tune what we are manifesting. There is nothing wrong with wanting to manifest something specific, but I do believe it makes people think that it is something to do when we have the time instead of it being something that is constantly happening.

People have the ability to make up reasons for their circumstances, like karma! 'I said this or that to this person or it must be that persons fault', but really, all we need to know is that we are a vibration. It could not have happened if we did not have our energy tuned into it.

We are a vibrational match to what we bring in and we bring many things in, in so many different ways. Whatever we ask for we get through different routes and depending on our vibration, we get it in different ways. If you want a new car but you are a match to a car accident rather than a winner in the lottery then the Universe can only give you what you want by matching your energy. The Universe always matches your vibe. We do not need to dwell on this though. We do not need to follow the path back to how something happened and why. It is more important to spend that time tuning up our energy to focus on what we want next. People tend to focus their energy of figuring out how they manifested something unwanted, but all they need to know is that the Universe is telling them that they need to tune up a little, that is all. It is not important to consider your past vibrations. If something negative has happened then this is because of a past vibration, not what is happening now.

Our inner being, our soul, is always trying to help us out and it never stops. I had a moment last week where my son kept nagging me to go out and get food. I was feeling a low vibration and told him I was not going anywhere but he would not quit. He wanted Chinese food for dinner and I kept telling him I was not going anywhere because I did not want to get in my car and drive anywhere at that moment. He finally gave up and left me in peace. Fifteen minutes later I started to get hungry myself and I got an intense desire to go get pizza so I finally gave in and decided to go on the drive. Distraction is great with lower vibrations. The minute I pulled out of the driveway and saw the sky I snapped back into alignment. It was at that exact moment that I realised the Universe was trying to get me out. It was using my son as a gift to me to try to help me bounce back but with no such luck, it went to my stomach!

The Universe is constantly trying to tell us what we want but we have to allow it to come to us. The Universe kept sending my son in but I kept pushing him away so the Universe decided to make me hungry instead. When I say our inner being is part of who we are, and the Universe is a part of who we are: this was just a great example. Clearly, when I was in that state of despair I was subconsciously asking for help so the Universe tried to help me out and did it in different ways, but I was asking for help and refusing it.

The minute we have a thought, the Universe has already thought it. For me, I daydream more than I visualise. It is emotional candy. I go and sit down with the intent of feeling really good and let the Universe handle the rest. I let the Universe feed me those good things. Daydreaming is an emotional ecstasy for me, whereas for some people it is an exercise. This is very different and it gives a different vibration. I would much rather have a slice of daydreaming ecstasy than a rigid routine.

Some days, I will be sitting at my desk and I will just stop for five seconds and return to who I desire to be. I punctuate my day with that. That desire of who I am stays with me. Not even who I want to be, who I am. We do not need to wait for that, just align with it. Throughout the day I align with it. I am this, I am that. Not what I am now, that is here. The version of who I want to be exists in a vibration somewhere, I just have to take time out to align with it. There is no need to create what already exists. When you are doing this you step into a different reality rather than create it. If we always went into those realms it would be a different story for all of us. If we all did that, everything would be very different.

To find more about Allison visit: ***allisonphillips.tv***

2
Living in Alignment

Alignment is living within the same vicinity as our souls. We are made of love as we are all created in the image and likeness of God, and when we live from the standpoint of love we create love in every area of our life. Our happiness is everything.

Many people ask me about alignment. They tell me that they live in alignment most of the time, or more often than not, but bad things still happen to them. When they tell me this I tell them that if they are experiencing bad things then they are not in alignment. This is not because when you are in alignment nothing bad happens, it means that when you are in alignment you realise that there is no such thing as bad. Bad things do not exist in love. They do not exist within our Universe, they exist only in our minds. We create things, we put labels on things. We say, "This is good and that is bad. This is pretty and that is ugly. This is okay and that is not." This is man made. When we are in alignment we see nothing as a problem because in our alignment we see the Universe working its magic.

The Universe is like a pendulum and the *Law of Rhythm* tells us that the pendulum is always swinging. It swings left the exact amount it swings right and it is always moving. It is because it vibrates as we do that we feel it, but we can feel it more depending on what frequency we are on. This is called the *Law of Vibration.* Everything within the Universe is constantly moving and nothing stops. When you live on a low frequency it always feels like you are being knocked about from left to right, but this is just because you are feeling the effects of the pendulum. When you live higher than this, when you live in alignment, you are above the pendulum and therefore you cannot feel it. You no longer feel those knocks because you are standing tall and you are above the beat. This is how the masters of our time live. They know that there is a vibrational rhythm to the Universe and they work around it.

When we are in alignment we see no bad, we only see things for what they really are—we see the lessons. Everything is a learning curve. Things are not put in front of us to hurt us or to knock us down, they are put there to give us opportunities to see our growth. This is the *Law of Relativity.* This law tells us that we have set tasks ahead of our life here on earth that will challenge us in order for us to grow. If we can go through our own versions of hell and continue to get through it whilst staying connected to God then we have mastered the self. We are not here to find out who we are, we are here to remember who we are.

When we are aligned without wants, needs and desires, we manifest things very quickly because we are feeling that oneness with the Universe. This is why it is so important to only take action when it feels good because we are then following the guidance of the Universe rather than our ego's.

The Journey to Love

I enjoyed every day and was grateful for every morning, every afternoon and every evening. I surrounded myself with people I loved and people who made me feel great. As the months rolled on I started visualising my life to come surrounded by great friends and a wonderful man. I did not visualise this to bring it to me, I visualised it only because it made me feel wonderful. Looking back I can see how aligned I was to the Universe because I spent everyday happy. I would drive to work and say in my mind, 'I have the most amazing husband, friends and family.' Eventually, this image of a handsome stranger became a familiar image in my mind. I saw a checked shirt and an impressive physique with thick hair that I could run my hands through and a sense of humour that always kept my cheeks rosy. Many times in my visions he would stop by for a cup of tea and ask for 'a real cup of tea made by a real English lady,' as he was not English himself. Sometimes I would imagine him busy at work in his office, sometimes I would imagine him relaxed and playing his guitar to me and sometimes we just danced in the rain in Central Park. One of my most popular visions was him and I walking through the park, dancing, talking, laughing and sometimes he would stop me in my tracks and sing to me. He adored me and his spirit made me fly. To me, he was real. He was so real that anytime

I felt down I would go to him in my mind. I remember a particular time that I was feeling incredibly sad and I was crying in my car on my way home. I relaxed myself and went within and poured my words out to myself. I spoke out all my feelings and frustrations, but I did it as if I was with him and telling him about my day. After I had done this I naturally visualised his response. He was so gentle with me, he was kind, he spoke to me with love and comforted me. To be honest, I did not even realise I was doing this because it just all came so naturally. Like I said, he was real to me and after he comforted me I felt a lot happier.

Then, one day, after having an inspiring conversation with my older brother, I decided to book a trip to New York City. It was a place I had been to a couple of times and have always wanted to eventually live once I found a way of doing so. After hanging up the phone with my brother I walked into my job that day and told my boss I would be leaving. Many people laughed at me, some told me I was irresponsible but I was making decisions with my heart now, not my head, and in that month my life changed once and for all.

On August 8, 2015, two weeks before I was due to fly, a message popped through on a social media website from a handsome gentleman in the United States. When I say handsome, I mean the most handsome man I had ever seen with the kindest blue eyes, the biggest smile and the most intoxicating laugh I had ever heard. After a brief chat, he wished me well and left the conversation. I was desperate to talk more. I did not know his name or where he was from but I wanted to. I wanted to know everything about him. It was not just how I felt about him, it was how he had made me feel through a few words we had shared back and forth. He had so much energy it was infectious.

The next day he reached out to me again. I was over the moon. The more he shared his life with me the more I realised how wonderful he was. He was kind, generous, ambitious, funny and he loved the Universe like I did. His name was Bobby. He was a business man doing extremely well in his field. He had toured in a band for many years previously and he still liked to play guitar and sing now and then when he had the time. He had written many beautiful songs and sang many to me. His voice was unique and totally perfect and I could barely listen to a song without feeling a rush of emotions.

When he asked me what was going on in my life I told him I was traveling to New York City for a month. He was so excited about the idea and keen to hear about my adventures. Within a couple of days he had asked me if he could fly over from where he was in San Diego and take me out because he thought it would be a shame if we never got to have lunch together. I was thrilled. We made immediate plans and within two days he had his flight and hotel booked and time off from his hectic job.

A week later there I was in an apartment on the Upper West Side, which was perfect and everything I had visualised. Three days after I landed he knocked on my door. I ran down to let him in and finally got to see those blue eyes in front of me. His trembling lips kissed me and it has been magic ever since. He spent five days with me before he flew back home and I was grateful for every minute. We explored the entire city on foot. We shared tasty food over storytelling and the driest wines we could find. One of my more memorable evenings was sitting at a beautiful restaurant enjoying Italian food and wine. After the meal was over he leaned in and asked if I wanted to walk with him to Central Park for a dance. I was beaming from ear to ear as we walked up one block to where the park was located. Here, we shared our first dance and as we did, it began to rain. There I was, dancing in the rain in Central Park just as I had visualised. It only rained for about three minutes. To me, it felt like the heavens had opened to allow me the moment I had once visualised where he and I were dancing in the rain under a tree in Central Park. I thank God for that moment still.

The very next day we were walking alongside the park again and he turned to me and asked if I liked the idea of getting married in Central Park. I was lost for words. This was something I had always wanted but never expressed to him. It was like a moment of perfect fate had brought us together, like he could read my thoughts, like I was stepping into my own self created future. Later that day he walked me to a spot in the park that he said would be great for a wedding. It was a busy area but we managed to find a spot to stand and enjoy the view. As we did this I heard some music playing in the background but not just any music. It was a piece of classical music that I used to play and visualise walking down the aisle to many years prior. Where was it coming from? I looked around to see a man playing the cello and playing this exact piece of music perfectly. All I can say is that I was absolutely stunned. Not only that, after pointing out how beautiful this music was to Bobby he then turned to me and said, 'I have always wanted this song played at my wedding. It would be perfect for you to walk down the aisle to.'

To this day he still asks for his cup of tea from a real English lady and I always say yes. Everything about him is what I visualised and nothing has been left out. This for me was my biggest moment of realisation that we can create exactly what we want and as long as we always go with thoughts of love we will always receive.

I believe that if I had not followed my instincts to leave my job and get on that plane then we may not have met. Our instincts are our inner being guiding us and our inner being never gets it wrong. One thing I have learned these last few years is to only make decisions out of love. Do not make haste. Do not make decisions out of fear or revenge or anger because sadly, they will not end well. Living in alignment will always bring you what you want.

3
We are all one

There is a law within our Universe called the *Law of Divine Oneness*. This law tells us to do to others as we do to ourselves, as we are all one soul. This is why it is so vital to take care of ourselves. When you look around at others you will see they can treat themselves as unkindly as they treat other people. We must love ourselves and treat ourselves well in order for the people around us to do the same. So many people talk to themselves with such unkind words that it is no wonder others do it to them. They pick themselves apart in front of the mirror, eat foods that are just posing as foods, rarely exercise, and if you give them a compliment about their appearance they think you are crazy and they choose not to believe you. Even worse, they think that you want something from them. This is such a toxic way to live and does not serve anyone. We are all perfect, we are all loved and we are all created in the likeness of God. What people fail to realise is that when they dislike themselves they are disliking God and the Universe. How can we expect the Universe to work so perfectly for us if we do not think we deserve it or if we disrespect it by disrespecting ourselves? So I say, let's love ourselves, hug ourselves, treat ourselves with kindness and we shall see that others will speak to us in the same way. Kindness shall rain upon you if you are kind to yourself. Never beat yourself up and never tell yourself you are wrong. You are not wrong. You are never wrong.

We must also remember that we are all one soul, we are all united and there is no separation. What you give out to the Universe you are also giving to yourself. If we speak harshly to one another we are not hurting the other we are hurting ourselves because that other individual is part of our unity.

If you want something for yourself then give it away. Whatever it is, give it away. If you want to be kind then be kind to others. If you want to be loving then love others. If you want to be gracious then be gracious to others. What we put out to the Universe always comes back to us, this is the *Law of Compensation.*

In this world today people do very little of this, not just because they want it all for themselves but because they believe they have little to offer, which is simply not true. When you tell someone to give what they have they immediately look into their pockets. This is because they are under the misapprehension that they are what they have. They think they are what they have earned, the car they drive, the house they live in. People think their material gain defines them and the more they have the happier they will be. This is why so many people are unhappy but cannot discover why. They think they must gather more stuff to make it happen yet it never does. This is because they have failed to look within themselves for their own happiness. When we go within and remember who we are we can begin to remember our power and our beauty and what we find inside we can then give to others. When we give to others the Universe instantly gives it back to us doubled. Whatever we want in life we must become the source of it. If we want more money we must give it away. If we want more love we must love others. When we are the source to these things the Universe sees this and gives us more of it so that we can continue on our mission to keep helping others.

You must give to receive and not for material gain but for gaining the knowledge of who you truly are. When you give to another love you connect to the Universe, you connect to your true self, leading to that blissful moment when you connect to the divine. There is nothing more fulfilling than giving and helping another and this can be in so many different ways. If a friend is down we can make them a hot drink and listen to them. If someone drops something then we can help them to pick it up. If we ask, the Universe will always provide opportunities for us to give to another.

The Journey of James Martin

Giving has always been a large part of my life because I recognise that it is my inner voice that I am hearing. My first experience with this voice was back in Junior High School. It was around lunchtime and I had this voice inside my head that told me to give this other student my lunch. I had seen him around and he usually had lunch with him and never looked like he was struggling for money or had any issues, but there was something about that moment that compelled me to reach out. As it happened, I had already eaten my lunch so I took him through the lunch line and bought him some food. I will never forget that because he chose pizza with nacho dipping sauce! I felt so good about giving that boy an opportunity to eat because I think that anyone who is hungry deserves to be given food. This has been part of my life ever since. I can be at the grocery store and I will hear this voice inside me telling me to buy someone's groceries or I will be driving down the road and this voice tells me to pull over and help somebody. I always listen to it now because first of all we are all connected and I believe I am being summoned by the Universe to play a part in the Universe's role, so it is not me that is doing this it is the Universe itself. Secondly, there will come a time where I hope that if I am ever in need someone will respond to the Universe and help me.

If you are open to your own self, to your intuition and to your higher self, then you are going to know when to and when not to give. I think that sometimes you can give a smile and you have changed somebody's life and you do not even know it. There are other things that are more tangible. For example, you have an apple in your hand and a thought in your mind tells you to not give it away but you do it anyway. Why did you do that? Was it because you did it due to your ego or because you wanted to feel good about yourself? If you have a voice that tells you not to do something then do not do it because it is not yours to give. Eat it and enjoy it, it is yours. It is your abundance. On the other hand, if you get a voice inside your head that says to give the apple away and you eat it then you have just eaten something that is not yours and you have robbed another of their abundance. Listen to the voice inside your mind that tells you to do good to somebody or give somebody something, including giving to yourself, because if that is the case then what you are holding no longer belongs to you. The more you listen to that voice the better discernment you will have.

I remember one time I was at the grocery store and I had this voice inside my head that told me to go and pay for this person's groceries but I did not want to. In fact, I was pretty adamant that I was not going to do this because I had been doing it all week and I wanted something for myself this time. I got out to my car and as I started driving away this voice inside my head seemed to release in a negative way. At that moment I felt like I had let myself and the Universe down so I turned the car around instantly and went back. Luckily, they were in line so I managed to go over and purchase their groceries for them. I felt so much better after that and from then on I always listen because it is not worth ignoring it.

Another blessing I had was at a restaurant where I had the opportunity to do the same thing. I offered to pay for somebody's food and the Universe instantly compensated me back and I ended up getting free food myself when the manager of the restaurant saw my generosity and compensated me for my meal: but the compensation does not have to be of a like kind. I once helped a man buy a jug of milk for three bucks and he totally broke down and asked if he could give me a hug. I had felt a little lonely that day and this experience filled me with warmth inside, so the emptiness that I was feeling that day was filled by him expressing gratitude and thankfulness. I always think it is a real shame when people say no to the Universe because you really do not want to lose that special gift or that special bond that you have with your inner being. It is God talking to you and you really want to listen to that.

I think that it is important to remember that nothing is really yours. It all belongs to the Universe. You cannot take it with you and you did not have it when you came here and it is going to return to someone else at some point because it will end up in a charity shop or in a landfill someday. The biggest piece of advice I would give to somebody is to give when you are compelled to give. Give if you have made a commitment to give. It feels good to give and sometimes it might stretch you but if you listen to your inner voice and you give then you are going to feel good about it and you will get confirmation in your soul that you are doing the right thing because it was not yours to begin with. Some people say give with a joyful heart, but I say give if your heart is joyful or not because the act and spirit of giving can bring a joyful heart. If you do not have a joyful heart and you give out of obedience or out of the practice of doing good for others then that will come to you and you will begin to feel that joy in your life.

As I continue to mature and grow into my own spirituality I am more conscious of the different laws, especially the Law of Attraction and the *Law of Compensation*. There are so many fundamental truths that I am more aware of now that I have grown. When I was younger I just wanted to do what was right and be a good man but now I want to also operate within the laws of the Universe where I can be blessed with my desires and add value to the world and be an even better man. When I give I never do it to get something back, I give to enrich, I give to help others. When I am stuck in a place I try to give more time so that I get more time out of life. If I am in a relationship with my special girl and I feel like I am not getting as much attention as I need then I give attention in hopes that it will come back to me in one form or another even if it is not from her but from all kinds of other people recognising my work or recognising my value. I am using the *Law of Compensation* more in my life now than I ever have done so in the past and I am going to continue to do so.

4
Showing Gratitude

Impatience is one of the more detrimental emotions that we can put out to the Universe. It says that we need something now to be happy. This then tells the Universe that we are not grateful for our current circumstance, we are not grateful for all that we have learned so far, or for the amount of soul growth we have experienced. Impatience is ungratefulness and we cannot get anywhere being ungrateful. We must cherish every moment.

Gratitude for everything is of the utmost importance, for it is on the same frequency as *love*. If anyone has tried to ask the Universe for something or prayed to God for something with no luck, then it is because there is little or no gratitude. We cannot ask from a place of not having and this is where so many get confused. To ask we must ask from the place of knowing. What many people tend to do is get to their wit's end and fall to their knees and pray to God for answers, for health, for wealth, for anything. This is coming from fear and therefore it cannot come. When we are desperate and asking for something it is because we are afraid of what will happen if we do not get it. This is not the place we want to ask from. We want to get to a place where we are so happy, so aligned that it makes little difference whether we have it or not. It would simply just be fun to have it. This is when the Universe starts moving for us. When we ask from a point of desperation the Law of Attraction can only bring more of that desperate feeling and what many people find is that when they are down about something more things start happening to make them feel worse. This is the Universe bringing to them more of what they are putting out.

We must appreciate what we have attracted whether it is good or bad because it was us that attracted it and the Universe brought it to us. This is why it is so important to look back and see how far we have come. Very few people do this because they have so many high expectations for themselves, whereas in reality they have probably grown in such large amounts that they can be a different person each week but not know it. It is important to take the time to appreciate yourself, what you have done and what you have created because gratitude is where the soul lives.

The Journey of Stephen Connor

Just before I moved into my awakening I was ready to take my own and my soul's life. I was totally ready to step away from it and I was seconds away from doing it. I rang my daughter and I was basically just going to say goodbye. After I got off the phone I thought to myself, 'What am I doing? I have got the ability to live a good and happy life. What is going on here?' I knew right then and there that if I wanted to live a happy life I had to change. It was as simple as that, it was a tipping point and the change or intentional inner growth, just keeps evolving.

The evolution of the soul is dependent on each individual's circumstances and the way this slowly transpires is wonderfully unique. It happens in levels and the time span is also very unique. This is important so we can develop our own inner rock and solid foundation for whatever life throws at us. This is the truth of who we really are and finding it is worth every ounce of effort.

There needs to be a lot of trust in this evolution or process. I did not quite listen enough to my inner voice in my process. I would say it took me about ten years to experience my own truth, which in turn brought inner peace, thankfully I was really committed to the process.

Along the journey, I have learned three things that are of most value to me: Confidence, Independence and Authenticity. You have to trust and believe in yourself to imbed these into your being, and along the way you have to be gentle with yourself. This is a really big part of it. You will see things that you probably will not like as you become more aware of your inner make up. You have to learn to turn this around, because as you see a part of yourself that you do not like or need to change, it is important to look at that part and love it and appreciate the fact that you know what to change to be a better person. It does take time for this to happen, so being gentle and appreciating the opportunity to better yourself makes the journey that much more enjoyable.

Because we all grow and evolve in our own unique way, I think we can get to the point of inner growth and clarity, whereby we want to just shake people and wake them all up. My advice here would be to let it go. Our inner magnet will do enough, our passion will do the work, our energy will help change the world. You will not change anybody. You can influence and inspire them but trying to change someone else is fraught with disappointments and as I found out, can lead to harsh reactions. The only person you need to change is yourself and in doing so the world will be a better place.

There is a reason for us to step away from trying to change others and that is to let people have their own go at it. They have to 'get it' in their own way. Our words will resonate with them, some more so than others, some the next day, others, twenty years from now, but they will remember us or the words in their own time.

I have a real appreciation for how I attract. It is not so much of wanting something but changing your thought patterns to more positive ones to allow it to come. When something comes to me, and my life gets better I say, 'I have attracted that.' For example, my next book is in the process of cover design. I had a woman come to me out of the blue and told me she was a designer and wanted to help me. She gave me a great price so I told her to throw some ideas at me. She did this but I could not decide which way to go so I told her that I trusted her. She came to me just at the right time, I attracted her, so I trusted that she would give me what I wanted.

The attraction comes after the event for me. When I was in the process of writing my second book, a biography, there were months of putting the transcription into a readable form. I was being paid well and so I gave up my normal job. I appreciated what I had created and saw the wonder in that. I had attracted this new life and I had money to do what I wanted. I wanted to travel. I wanted to get work done on my house and now I could do it all.

If there is something that would benefit me I do not create a plan but things just seem to happen. I then stand back and look at what I attracted and I just love that. I am a very easy going, minimalistic kind of guy and it took a lot of trust, knowing and experience to believe in myself and the fact I had attracted something. It also took appreciation and confidence in myself to offset the doubts of attraction.

I find that it is important not to rely solely on attraction. You cannot say that you want something and then just wait. That is the downfall for some people. They want something and so they visualise it and then just wait for it to be handed to them. They do not realise the important element of putting the effort in to attract it to themselves. They think it will just come. The effort is more important than the outcome. Relying on the material and external is temporary and fleeting, the internal is where the benefits of attraction happen.

The Law of Attraction is a way to describe the potential magnet that is within our bodies: that is where the attraction happens. As you evolve, you have the old you and the new you. You can feel your awareness and your appreciation change as you work towards the new. The old still presents itself. Things happen to you and your inner magnet. The new you experiences life differently to the old you and you love it and want more, it is empowering. You do not rely on it because it just happens, this is the eternal magnet you have to keep powering up and loving it.

To find more about Stephen visit: *stephenconnor.org*

5
Contrast within the Universe

Contrast is one of the most powerful ways in which we can create but it is also one of the most powerful ways we can step on our own toes, therefore perspective is key, after all, every cloud really does have a silver lining. When we experience something that we find extremely displeasing we are instantly asking the Universe for the exact opposite. We create through our contrast and this contrast within the Universe is based around the *Law of Polarity*. This is seen at its best in relationships. Many of us have had very fulfilling relationships and some of us have had extremely detrimental ones that make us feel tired or worn out. This is contrast at its best.

By experiencing such relationships we are then asking the Universe for something different. We are naturally emitting that power of wanting the opposite. If we get into a relationship where someone is particularly suffocating, jealous or needy, then we experience more of that from this person because the Law of Attraction keeps bringing us more. The more we notice something and focus on it the more we get of it. However, we are setting forth new desires of wanting the opposite. We may not realise it but we are gradually creating the idea of the perfect partner within our subconscious mind and as soon we are able to align with our inner being we can set forth towards that new person.

This can be extremely difficult for many to get their head around but it is caused by their mindset. When we live in a world that does not understand this powerful Law of Attraction then life events seem somewhat random and uncontrollable. People see things as accidents and despair over them, worry about them and do not realise that the Universe is giving them more of it. The energy that we put out we receive back. The Universe does not see negative or positive energy it just creates more of whatever it already has.

The reason things can seem stagnant or displeasing sometimes is probably because they are. Our inner being is always growing and expanding through this contrast. It takes everything and sees the next positive step forward, but the problem is that instead of taking these lessons under our belts and running with them we are complaining that they are too heavy to carry. We hear it all the time—people complaining about the money they lost, the coffee they spilled, a spouse that has left. The complaint is a pure disbelief of a higher power, of our Universe at large. It is a disallowing of something better and of something more. If we complain more than we appreciate, then life will never seem to go the way we want it to.

The more that the negative is focused on the more it grows and this does not take long. According to Abraham Hicks, if we focus on something for as little as seventeen seconds another thought like it comes forth. This is wonderful if we are not creating by default, but if we are creating by default it is detrimental to us. Soon, after focusing on that one negative thought, one exactly like it, which we dislike just as much then joins it. This is followed by another and then another. This is how people tend to spiral down their emotional scale and end up feeling powerless and depressed. They have totally sunk themselves and it can be tough to swim back up to the surface. This entire experience did not have to happen if we all knew the bigger picture or if we all trusted that there is more out there for us.

We learn from contrast. We create from contrast and we ask from contrast. If we focus our perspective on the good, the wanting, the opportunities; we shall never have room for the egotistical version in which we have created and we will only see infinite abundance. There is also a bigger picture, more to the story, we are just in one paragraph but there is an entire book to read. It is so important to appreciate every moment for what it holds and what it can create for us because it is always leading us somewhere. Is it not more fun to be surprised? Besides, if we know the benefits of our creation we must know that all we create is positively magical.

My own experience of Contrast

Polarity, meaning contrast, was and still is one of our toughest lessons to come to terms with. Many of us, including myself, think that we make mistakes or that we wish we did something differently. It has taken me a few years to really accept my life as it is and forgive myself or my 'mistakes'. After all, they are not mistakes, but are lessons learned and new desires launched into our cosmic Universe. I have learned to be kind from being unkind. I have learned to listen from years of talking too much and I have learned to be still from too much restlessness.

I remember not too long ago I had one of my biggest moments of contrast. I had spent many months meditating, exercising, trying to eat well, follow my intuition and just learn every step of the way. I was learning more and more about who I was, or should I say, I was *remembering* who I was.

At this time I decided it would be a wise decision to go on the contraceptive pill. I had been on it before many years ago but it had been about six months since I had taken it. It was not my first choice but I weighed up all the other options and this seemed to be the lesser of the two evils so after a few weeks of going back and forth I decided to do it.

Everything seemed to be going fine when suddenly, after about five days of taking it, I started observing my thoughts and emotions and did not like what I was seeing. Instead of my mind going to the positive in every situation it went to the exact opposite. My mind started creating fear instead of love and it started to really get to me. Within two days I was the lowest I had ever felt. After those couple of days my body naturally started going along with what my thoughts and actions were doing and I lost all my energy. I could not sleep at night and could not get up during the day. I was exhausted. I was scared. I did not want to leave my home and when I did I felt utter panic. This was not the real me and I had to do something to change that. This is the first and only time I have ever experienced the opposite end of the spectrum where I based my life and I was totally out of my depth. For the first time I had little faith in myself, I felt lost and I felt lonely. The reason I felt lonely was because I could no longer hear God. My connection to the Universe was completely pinched off and I was left there in what felt like ordinary mundane life with no guidance.

It took me those couple of days to come to the conclusion that it was the pill that had created something in me that was not favourable, so I decided to immediately stop taking it, but there was still a part of me that was scared. I hoped that when it left my system I would be back to normal, but what if I had to do it myself and pick myself up off the ground. I had never felt so powerless in my life before and this was a whole new learning opportunity for me.

This was one of the biggest moments of contrast I have ever experienced. Not only did it make me appreciate how amazing I felt within the next week but it also made me realise how far I had come and how connected I was normally. I never wanted to question my growth again. I took deliberate steps forward to bring me back to my centre. There were three things that I had been wanting to do for a while but had not. For what reasons I cannot tell you for I do not know, maybe laziness? For whatever reason, I had been ignoring my intuition on these things and I felt that this was the best opportunity for me to take action in those things. These three things were becoming vegan, doing morning yoga and praying.

I took action immediately and I have never looked back. This moment of clarity has been one of the biggest moments in my life so far. It has given me such appreciation for my connection to God and to the Universe and it makes me so excited to have come this far. Since this time I have had many people come to me and tell me about their depression, their powerlessness, their guilt, and I feel like my empathy is strong because of what I have learned from my own experience. After all, what is more beautiful than to lose oneself in order to once again find oneself?

6
Asking for what you want

Asking the Universe for what we want is our first step in our creation and a very important one. Once you have asked, you must then go forward to receive it. Since the Law of Attraction has become so well known over the years many people have forgotten its counterpart—*the Law of Action.* This law is reminding us that we have to take action with our desires in order to receive them. This action should be taken in joy, it should feel fun and inspirational. If it is not then the Universe is guiding you elsewhere.

There are two ways in which we can ask—we can ask for something consciously or subconsciously and either way, we receive it every time. If we know we are in a world of such creation then we must therefore know what we create has to first be affirmed. We may not realise it but we are always asking every second of the day and this is through that contrast we just talked about. If we eat a bad apple we are subconsciously asking for cleaner food. If we step on a small rock we are subconsciously asking for a smoother path. If we are becoming inundated with phone calls and emails we are subconsciously asking for an assistant. This is constant whether you know it or not. The only problem that arises here is that instead of people experiencing it and appreciating what they have learned in order to now ask for what they want, they spend their time complaining about the contrast and therefore never receive what they have learnt to really desire. When you go to a cash machine and see that you do not have enough money for your bills you are subconsciously asking the Universe for more money but that money will never come because you are now telling your friends that you cannot afford to pay your heating bill or that you are struggling to pay for your groceries. You then go home and tell your other half that you are worried and that you are both going to struggle this month. You then tell your children that they have to be careful that month with hot water or putting on the heating because the bills need to be reduced to fit your current state of affairs. Before the Universe has had time to create something for you that you have asked for, you have crushed it.

This is why it is so important to see contrast as it is—it is just clarity. It is just telling us that we need to ask for something in order to receive it rather than tell the world what we lack. We have an entire Universe on our side, we just need to learn how to appreciate that.

When we ask for it consciously, we are purposely and deliberately using our words and our powerful thoughts to ask for something specific. We can ask for more money, a better relationship, better food choices, a warm home. There is an infinite amount of things to create within this Universe and we shall never run out, for the journey ignites more ideas within us. We shall always ask. What we want to learn is from that contrast that we just experienced or it is by seeing something that we enjoyed. This is where our emotions are key. The world that we see around us is a catalogue. We see beautiful homes, fancy cars and acres of land. Within those things we see different types of people wearing different types of garments. Some are wearing luxurious jewellery and designer clothes. Some are drinking expensive drinks and dining at the best restaurants. Some are talking about their well paid jobs or enjoying their joyful family and friends. Literally, everything is a catalogue and this is why we need to learn to keep our emotions in check. It is very important to allow ourselves to become sensitive to the way we feel because the way we feel is the way we are creating. If we see someone that has what we want it does not mean that they can have it and we cannot. In fact, the person that has that car you want had to have seen it elsewhere in order to ask the Universe for it in the first place. We can always have what we want but it is up to us to ask for it. If we see someone that has what we would like, then it is important to feel gratitude towards them for allowing you to make another request to the Universe.

Unfortunately, what most people do is feel jealous. They feel deprived and therefore the Universe cannot bring it to them. Even worse, they talk themselves out of it because it feels better to do that than to 'accept' that they cannot have it. They tell themselves or their friends that they do not want to be rich, they just want to be comfortable. They tell themselves and their friends that they do not want that large cozy family home, they are happy as long as they have just a roof over their heads. They tell themselves and their friends that they do not want that fancy car, they are happy taking the public transport This may well be true for some but for others this is due to thinking that they cannot have it and that they will never receive it. People put other people on pedestals and think that certain things are unreachable, but they are not. Naturally, instead of wanting and it not coming, they get to a level of accepting that they shall never have it and therefore they never will. It is important to see what you want and ask. You do not need to know how you will receive it, it does not matter. That is not your job. It is the Universes job to bring it to you. Your job is to just ask.

Action is important when it comes to asking because our actions must line up with what we are wanting or who we are trying to be. If we want to lose some weight but then go to a dinner party and choose an unhealthy meal then our actions are not lining up with our desires. However, if we choose an option that is better for us then we are lining up with our desires. Our thoughts, words and actions need to line up as often as possible in order to receive what it is we are asking for.

My Asking List

I decided it was time to find a part time job as my other commitments were coming to an end and it felt only right to leave it to the universe to decide what job was appropriate for me at the time. One night a friend popped into my head. I had worked with her for a few years and she was a wonderful employer. Going with my gut instinct I decided to call her to see if she had any work but she did not. She did however, know of a job in the same company but a different location which she said she would be happy to recommend me for. After a few days I had an interview under my wing.

The night before my interview I wrote down how I wanted the day to unfold. This was a method I had learned from my trusty Abraham Hicks book. I was basically telling the Universe how I wanted my day to go and this was the first time I was to put it into practice. My list said the following:

1. *A great parking space*
2. *Part time working hours to be offered to me*
3. *A kind boss*
4. *Free coffee*
5. *£100*
6. *New shoes*

I put 'new shoes' at the end of my list for two reasons—it made me laugh and I love shoes! That morning I awoke early.

I picked out my favourite vintage pale blue Versace suit to wear to my interview. I scanned my dozens of shoes that were in neat rows across my wardrobe floor. I thought a deep navy would go beautifully, but much to my surprise, I did not own a navy pair so I went with nude. I pulled them out of my closet leaving a neat gap in my row of stilettos. I then threw on a pair of sandals to drive in and left the house. I jumped into my car to make my journey and I left in plenty of time so I could be there early. When I arrived I looked at the clock and saw that I was earlier than I had anticipated because the traffic was as perfectly calm as I was. I decided to make a dash for the store and pick myself up a snack to eat whilst I waited. As I parked, I turned off my engine, grabbed my handbag and went to step out of the car. As I did so I saw a flash of bright pink glitter run across my vision. It was my sandals. I could not walk in wearing them so I reached around my seat to grab my heels. They were not there. I looked all around the inside of my car until it dawned on me that I had left them behind when I grabbed my keys. It was early so only a handful of shops would be open but I knew I had an hour to rectify this. I started up my engine and headed towards one store that I imagined would likely be open and sold women's shoes at a good price. As I drove down the high street I saw a parking space right outside this store. I pulled in and jumped out and walked towards the doors. As I did so I saw a pair of shoes in the corner of my eye in a secondhand store next door to my intended destination. They were deep navy, patent, with a three inch heel. They were perfect. The store was open so I walked in and picked them up from the window display and took them to the desk. I did not even look at the size because I knew they were for me. I handed them over along with the eight pounds that they were being sold for. I took them back to my car and slipped them onto my feet. It was a Cinderella moment for sure. I laughed to myself as I drove down the road to my interview in my new navy shoes. There was a parking space right outside when I arrived. I stepped out and walked across the road. As I walked in, the manager was standing there in front of me with long wavy bleach blonde hair, a warm smile and a professional stance. She greeted me kindly and asked if I wanted to go to a local coffee shop for the interview. She bought me a coffee and we sat down. The interview went great and she set me at ease with her kind presence. She told me that if I was offered the job it would be part time hours for the time being but more if I ever needed them. We seemed to get on great and after working there for a year she is still one of my best friends today and a lover of the Law of Attraction.

I arrived home with a big grin on my face. I knew I would be offered that job and my day had gone just as I asked it to. As I walked into my house, my partner at the time was counting cash. He handed me one hundred pounds. He had been given a little extra that week for great work and he wanted to share it with me. Of course, later that day I felt around under my pillow case and pulled out the list from under it. I smiled and put a tick next to all five of my wishes and ticked the sixth wish two days later when I was officially offered the job. I have been a lover of lists ever since.

7
Emotional Healing

It is my belief that our divine purpose on this earth is simply this: *to learn to live in full connection to our true selves and remember who we are.* Our true selves meaning our alignment. There are many lessons out there which we are put through, many different situations and all of them are there for the same reason. We must learn to stay true to our selves and act with love through all of it. This is why our emotions are so important to us in these trying times because they tell us if we are on track or off track to our own divine purpose. We can tell where our emotions are by seeing what is around us, not just how we feel inside.

We attract the energy that we put out to the Universe. If we are practising the feeling of anger then we attract angry people. If we are practising the feelings of positivity then we attract positive people.

The Universe will always lead us to circumstances where we can practice that emotion. If we are angry then the Universe shows us more to be angry at. If we are positive then the Universe will show us more to be positive about. This is why those trying times in life are so beautiful. They are there to show us how connected we are and also, how much more we are connected than before. If anger is something we are working on then we will continue to be surrounded by circumstances that make us angry. This is because firstly, it is in our vibration and so we shall receive more of it, and secondly so that we can act on it and see how much we have grown. If we find ourselves still getting angry then we are not seeing growth; but if we are getting angry less often, or not as angry, or just frustrated, then we are growing closer to our connection with the divine. This is the *Law of Relativity*. This law tells us that certain things happen for a reason as a way to see how connected we are to our divinity. If we are always feeling positive and acting on thoughts of love then we are connected, and if we live connected, we live our life happily.

Many dislike change. They want things to stay as they are and have always been and so they always shall. We do not have to create if we do not wish, but creating is our natural state of being and so if we stop ourselves creating positively we stop ourselves from living a truly fulfilling life. Everything that we see around us is a creation. It may be our own creation or it may be that we have stepped into an environment where we are surrounded by other people's creations, but they are all one, they are all creations and they all started from one significant thing—a thought. Our thoughts are extremely powerful. Not necessarily the thoughts themselves but what the thoughts become. They become things. They do this when we attach emotions to them and this is easily done and also very hastily done for when we think we feel and when we feel we create. One small thought can enter our minds and not appear again for several days, but the more it pops up and smiles at us the more we smile back or frown back if that is the case, it eventually gathers momentum. When we put energy into it we start really feeling it and this is when creation starts. If we feel a positive emotion towards it, if it feels pleasurable, exhilarating, or exciting, then we are on our way to creating something extremely wonderful; but if we are feeling negative emotion about something and we are feeling very uncomfortable about it or jealous, or angry, or disempowered, then we are going down a path that shall be most displeasing to us. This is where one of the biggest confusions comes with learning about the Law of Attraction. When people start creating more specifically and still do not have things that show up in their lives they then turn back to disappointment because they have not yet realised that they must continue to look within to see what they like around them. They say that they could not have manifested an illness because they would never think of that illness or they say they could not have manifested that accident because they would never think of an accident. The sooner we all realise that we create everything including the bad, the more we can learn to find that balance. We are always manifesting. We do not need to learn how to do it because it is always happening, whether you believe it is or not. What we do need to learn is to focus our energy in the right direction.

We cannot use our emotions to stop momentum, we can only change the course. We cannot stop something, only look elsewhere. When we have a thought or a situation that we are not enjoying we can do two things. We can continue to think about it and allow it to grow or we can focus on something that we do enjoy and therefore not allow the negative to grow. It can take some time to create such habits for we have been born into a time where we will naturally learn positive and negative emotions and put labels on each thing, which is where it shall stay but it does not have to be like this. As I said, we are creators and we can create infinite abundance with just a subtle little thought. A thought creates money. A thought creates mansions. A thought creates mirthfulness.

We are now at a beautiful time where we can choose to create to our full potential without anyone holding us back. We can surround ourselves with those who know their creative worth and those who wish to build as we do and create as we do, for they know, as we do, that there is no better time to create than in this present moment.

Part of creating involves creating one's self. Everyone reflects us and we reflect them so there is contrast all around us. If we look at someone in front of us and the attitude they have towards us whether it be kind or unkind, we can always see ourselves within that. In fact, some of you may have even said before or heard some say to you that the reason you do not get along with another is because you are both exactly the same. You clash. The reason this feels so bad is because we literally have someone in front of us showing us our true colours and we do not like it. This is an important stage for us and we can fight back, we can argue, we can kick and scream and create dislike towards that person or we can look closer, see ourselves and take steps to change. The people around us tell us where we are emotionally for we cannot meet an angry person without having anger within us.

Discovering my own Emotions

I think our emotions are really important to us, but I think that people tend to shy away from them because they are unsure of how to deal with them. People are always distracting themselves from the pain that they feel by doing little things like watching television, cleaning or going out every evening. They do not realise that they are doing this but they are doing it all the same and I was one of them. For me, I do not believe I purposely pushed my emotions away but I used different things to distract myself. This was all with good intentions because I thought that if I wanted to use the Law of Attraction I had to stay positive and stay happy. It was well intentioned and I would distract myself, be happy and focus elsewhere, but at the end of the day these things kept emerging and I got to the stage where I realised that they were not going to go away. My fears have been with me a long time and I was still dealing with them. I was told by many people that I had problems with my anger. My previous relationships had sparked concerns and my current one was no different. What I finally realised was that this was the Universe telling me what I needed to work on.

One day I decided that I needed to look at this indepth because it felt like I was just brushing it under the rug and it clearly was not working for me, because my emotions were never stable for very long and it was exhausting. I was getting signs from the Universe about emotional healing and inner child work so I finally decided that it was time to take a look at myself indepth.

We create mind patterns as children. If we experience anything that is not to our pleasing (bearing in mind that as children we are pure positive light) then we feel the uncomfortableness of it. If you look around you will see a lot of children wipe their frowns away and put on a smile which all seems rather lovely, but what that can actually do is teach a child not to feel their negative emotions and mask any sadness they may be feeling. This then creates habits in an individual where they do not know how to deal with any painful emotions.

When I started to really look at my emotions and heal myself I never felt like I was forcing myself to do this. I could not have been more ready for this moment. I really allowed myself to feel my emotions and what I did was I would just sit with myself. Sometimes I would lie down in meditation, sometimes I would just wrap my arms around myself and sway from side to side and I would just feel that pain and be one with it in that moment. I was actually surprised how nice it was to feel the pain and then to feel the release of it. I never cut myself short, I never distracted myself or walked away, I stayed there in that moment with that emotion. I felt it until it no longer hurt. I did this many times and still do. If I get upset about a situation I turn into myself and ask myself why I am feeling the way I do. One of the best lessons I have learned is to not project my emotions onto another for it is not their fault. They are a reflection of what I am feeling and therefore blaming them will make it worse. What I need to do is ask myself why I feel the way I do and what I can do to comfort myself.

When I first started doing this I took time out for myself and I noticed that every few hours I would feel this pain and I believed it was my inner child wanting attention, so I would nurture her and feel her. I would do anything to comfort her and make her feel safe. The more I did this the less she wanted my attention. In time, when these things came to my mind they did not hurt so much and there was no longer any lingering pain in my body. When there is no lingering pain in the body then you are less likely to lash out and lose control. From now on if I feel the pain I stay there and feel it. I never brush it under the rug.

I finally saw the light a week after I began this when I failed to answer some calls from Bobby one afternoon. He was worried about me and not being able to get hold of me made it worse. When I did get to my phone he spoke to me with such tenderness and care that it was like I was talking to myself. He spoke to me like I spoke to me and from then on I knew it was working. He was reflecting my own self back at me and I realised then how important it is to take care of myself so that others can take care of me. If you love yourself then others can love you too.

I am taking the time to respect my mind and my thoughts and allowing them to tell me something. They are not telling me 'you are upset,' they are telling me, 'you are upset about this *because'*. It is the 'because' that I am healing. To remember who I am I must look at who I have become and correct it. I think that when you look at the Law of Attraction, if you get to the point when you want to focus on the good things then you may need to make room for them. You have to allow the bad things to leave in order to bring in better. People use the Law of Attraction as a surface thing but there are twelve universal laws and they all have their own place. People forget this because the Law of Attraction has been popularised over the years and has taken first place, but then other things get left behind. The things that get left behind are the things that are so important—oneness, unity and one with God. People tend to concentrate on manifesting material things. You have to be whole to manifest everything that you want. There is more to it than feeling like you have it, acting like you have it, imagining that you are getting all these things. If it is not working it is because something is blocked. Bad energy, bad thoughts, pain and suffering that you are holding onto is going to stop them from manifesting. When you are going through pain and brushing it under the rug you are putting up walls and blocking it. It is so important to release them in order to bring things in. What is actually happening is that you have asked for something and the Universe has started to try to give it to you instantly like it does. It will guide you to it but if the path is blocked it is going to lead you to healing first. If you have pain, suffering, anything in you that is not whole it is going to lead you to find self recovery first, so you can bring in the things that you have asked for. What many people feel is that they have asked for something, been happy for a while, not received it and now feel really disappointed. Why are you feeling disappointed? Is it because you did not get your own way? Is it because you demand it now?

Knowing what I do now, I absolutely encourage anyone to just feel whatever they are feeling and not be afraid of it. Whatever the pain is, it is there for a reason and it is not there to attack you, bring you down or to test you, it is there to be heard and dealt with. Once you have dealt with it and released it, it will start to unblock itself. This is an ongoing journey and we are always healing. There will always be things coming up and that is okay because the more you do it the easier it becomes. I used to feel a negative emotion and panic. I never knew what to do with it and then I ran from it and it created itself into more.

If you purposely push down on it then it will still create. You must accept it and let it go. This has been one of the most amazing parts of my journey because I have lived many years of ups and downs, and even in my awakening it was more extreme and I hoped it would balance itself out, which it did not, not completely. It did a little but not enough. I surrendered to the Universe and I looked for the answer and the answer that came to me was this:

You have to heal yourself first and you have to feel the pain and only when you feel the pain will you feel its release. It is not the other way around. You cannot distract from it. You cannot turn away from it. You cannot leave it behind. You have to feel it. However long it takes to let it go, just do it. If it comes back, feel it again. Wait it out and release it once again.

This is how the Universe communicated with me. I am now communicating it with you. If you are up and down all the time and feeling negative emotions about something, feel it, feel the reason for it and let it leave. Do not ignore it. You will feel so much lighter. You are no longer holding onto it and it is a liberating feeling.

To me, this is God's greatest gift and I will be forever grateful for receiving it. For the first time in my life I was not looking for any other way to mask my pain. I asked God to guide me and I was guided. I am forever grateful."

8
The Perfect Timing

I came to discover and so I will share with you all that there is no such thing as time. Time is an illusion. It is a tool that we have made in order to make sense of what happens around us and it is greatly appreciated in day to day life but unfortunately, it has made many of us weary. We try to beat the clock, we try to turn back the clock, we think we must do things by a certain time, we pressure ourselves unnecessarily and over time we have lost that connection with God and with the Universe. When we think that we have to beat the clock we push against that fast current that makes up our Universe which then stops manifestations coming our way. We tell God that we do not trust it will be with us on 'time' and so we try it out ourselves and this is exhausting.

When we think about time as being linear it certainly makes manifesting easier because what we are asking for what has already happened. When we affirm something to the Universe we are simply choosing a chapter out of all the different chapters we have available to us and stepping into it. We are literally lining up with something that has already happened.

Every second that makes up our 'time' is perfect in every way. It is up to us and our perspective to see it that way. We must know that everything happens for a reason and relax, let it happen. When we observe what is going on around us we certainly appreciate it more, and if we look back at our life so far we can see that things did in fact happen just at the right time.

It is very easy for people to see that what they are asking for is yet to reach them and for them to blame fate, blame God, or blame anything in the Universe that they think may be against them simply because it may feel easier than taking ownership and admitting that there is just not something that they understand about the Universe and about life. In my years of teaching I have had countless people ask me why God does not want them to have a specific person in their life or to make more, have that house, have anything nice? This is not God deciding for them because God's will is our will and what we want, God wants for us. The Law of Relativity however, does indeed work with us when it comes to certain pillars in our lives. Before we were born we set these here as lessons to go through, to encourage us to learn something in particular. We choose our parents and the place we wish to grow up in along with the environment. This is all for the purpose of growth, but when it comes to life's little decisions, these are up to us.

The Universe certainly does not tell us what we should or should not have, this is our responsibility. If something has yet to manifest into physical form it is because we are failing to allow it to blossom, we are being impatient or we think we need it to be happy. Need is an illusion within society. The illusion tells us we must have something now and if we do not have it we shall remain unhappy. This is true for many people who have looked at the outside for happiness. People who have tried to find joy in money, possessions or just 'stuff' will probably tell you it is not there. If it is not there then there is only one other place it can be—here. Within us is our joy, our happiness, our abundance. The Universe is within us, we are the Universe. We do not need to look anywhere for joy because we already have it built within us but we need to clear our minds to hear it.

Wisdom from the Other Side

I started seeing the spirit of my late Grandad when I was just fourteen. Since then, the world around me has changed and now not only do I get to see life through my physical eyes, I get to see them through the eyes of someone who is there on that other side, watching over me and observing the life that I am choosing to currently live. He, along with many other spirits of the night, have given me their wisest words. I would like to share some with you here.

One of the many things I have learned is that there is no right or wrong answer. You have certain things that you were born to do in your life, but how you get there is totally your choice. People get so caught up in the worries of whether they are making the right or wrong decisions, but it is important that you make the decision that is right for you at the time so you can look back and know that you made the perfect decision for the circumstances you were in.

It is to my knowledge that there are a few set pillars that people must come across in their life that they put there before they are born. This could be certain people who are meant to meet because together they will do amazing things or go through a certain experience because it will be a valuable life lesson which will roll onto greater things.

I have learned that people have certain tasks in their life that they have to accomplish, but it is your life's journey to get there, so you *will* get there. It is inevitable. These things, however, are bigger than you, so as long as you do what is right for you and you are not hurting anyone on the way then there is no reason why good things will not manifest for you.

If you have asked for guidance from the Universe then you have to be open minded to the small details. There could be a reason you went to that supermarket instead of your normal one, or that a friend canceled your Friday night dinner plans. These are all little steps guiding you to where you have asked to go so do not be afraid to stray from your routine.

To an extent, everyone is guided. Do something that lights a spark in you because those things are always the best for you. Do anything that makes your heart happy because that is what your soul needs. It is the only way to keep yourself in tune. For me, it is as small as having my cup of coffee in bed in the morning, a class at the gym and a good book. Once you get to that point where it is more within your soul then you will find guidance. If you find happiness then everything you desire will come to you. It really will.

I realise that trying to be positive all the time is sometimes shooting for the stars. Negative things will still show up but it is how you deal with them that matters. When this happens, be angry, get annoyed, if you have to cry then do so, but do not linger. Have your ten minutes but then let it go. For some, it is difficult to see a positive in a negative, but that is because you have to wait and ride the wave and see what glory comes out of it. They will always lead to better and also lead to your growth as a soul.

One night, an elderly man appeared to me and told me that life is too short to do things that you do not want to do. Do something that scares you instead. Do not look back at a wasted life. If you are not learning these lessons then your soul cannot go on to greater things. You need to do these things to learn or you will have to use more lives after this one to try again, so why not figure it out now?

Comfortable does not make change. Are you doing things in your day that scare you to help your soul grow and if not, why not start now? Look at your life and your routine and ask yourself if you are happy.

When it comes to manifesting and trying to bring in what you want, I would first ask why you want them. People tend to compare their chapter with other peoples despite what chapter each person is on. I left school a year early because I struggled too much and by the time I had battled home schooling I looked back on my life and felt totally left behind. All my friends were getting ready to go to college and university and I felt like I had nothing to show for myself. A lot of my friends now have finished their studies and are looking for jobs. I am still studying and looking forward to finding the right university for me. I have learned to focus purely on my own achievements and myself. I know my circumstances and I know how far I have come.

If you are at the age where your friends are getting married, having children or buying houses, something inside says that you must be doing that too and if you are not then you are a failure.

Take those people out of your thoughts for a minute and think, are you happy? Do you want things that others have because you do not have them? If you are trying to manifest something for the wrong reasons it will not come until you are ready. You will not manifest a relationship because you are fed up with telling others that you are single or because you want someone else to bring in the money so that you have a safe environment to leave your job. You will bring in the relationship when you get to a place of wanting their companionship, someone to grow with, learn with and love upon. Someone who supports your sparkle. Things will come to you when you find yourself.

I think the two most important things for your soul to learn are gratitude and appreciation. When you see negative, find the positive. Even if it is the smallest thing. If you are happy because the sun is shining and you love the heat then you must latch onto that. Look forward to sitting in that sun on your lunch break and reading your favourite book. Enjoy every minute of it. If you can come up with just three things to be grateful for before you go to bed at night then life can become good for you and it does wonders for your soul. If you have gone home to bed, be grateful for that bed. If you made yourself dinner, be grateful you have food. If you drove home, be grateful that you fuelled that car. There is an overall idea of being the perfect soul and being accepting of other human beings, loving other human beings and getting joy out of bringing people up rather than pushing them down. Grandad used to say to me, 'Do not set others on fire to keep yourself warm.'

I think it is important to be a soul of your own and to get through life trusting your own instincts and loving yourself. Loving yourself means everything. This is why a lot of people as they get older, look back and wish they had done a lot more and trusted themselves more. This is something that perhaps comes with age, so the sooner we learn it the better our lives will be.

9
Finding Freedom

The *Law of Perpetual Transmutation of Energy* is a law that tells us we have the ability to turn our lives around using our thoughts. We are all freedom seeking beings and it is our right to seek such freedom, but sadly too many experience the control of others. Not only that, they deem to control their own selves in a way that is not serving to their higher power. They do not step outside of the versions of themselves they have created because they do not want to be laughed at or judged. People tend to stay within the idea of themselves which can eventually become very tiring. It is also the same for us when we allow others to control and dictate to us what we do and how we do it. This is so unnatural to the soul that it becomes painful if it is carried out for long lengths of time. Eventually, we really lose our true selves when we do this.

This is what often happens in relationships because love can be conditional when we use our ego rather than using our own hearts. We see couples having rules within the relationship to make the other happy and when you see that control it is due to pain. When we get into a conditional relationship we bring that pain with us and feel the need to control another to make sure they do not do anything to cause more pain. This is why relationships like this tend to go two ways. They either end or both individuals become lost.

When an individual carries that pain within them they attract like minded individuals, because when we are constantly following the path of fear we can only attract fear— we can only ever attract what we are carrying. When two individuals meet with that same energy it may feel like they have finally met their soulmate, the 'one' and the relationship feels amazing but soon the control becomes too much. The beauty of this is to see our reflection and change our ways. We cannot live in such negative circumstances for so long because we are naturally loving beings and living in such negativity is just too painful so we seek more. We seek what feels best and although what is best may still be a negative emotion it will always be an emotion that was better than the last. If we are constantly attracting relationships and finding ourselves slipping into old ways of controlling the other and using fear and anger, or any other negative emotion to keep them, then we have not yet learned that this is not our way forward. We should not have to fight to keep someone with us. If they do not wish to stay then allow them the courtesy to leave and wait for someone who does want to stay. However, when we get into this momentum it is hard to get out unless we allow ourselves time to heal from it. We all see it every day where people hop from one relationship to the next not wanting to experience their own pain, hoping that the next person will make it fade away, but later on the same pattern emerges and off they go again. This is because it is still in our vibration, it never left because we never let it. Healing is so important and to do this we must travel alone sometimes. Otherwise, if we do not, we only attract the same type of relationship over and over again.

Not only do we see the control in relationships but parent and child too. Parents, through no fault of their own, can teach their children to please them and do things in order to make their lives easier and more peaceful. They tell their children to clean their room and they do. This is great because it teaches responsibility, but who are they cleaning their room for? Usually, it is for the parent. The parent asks them to do so and they do so with a big smile on their face and the children are so proud and excited for their parent to see the glistening room. This is so beautiful to see but why not teach them to clean it for themselves? If we teach them that a clean room is a way of respecting their own space, a way to feel nice and have clear energy around them, then they would be teaching them to go within and do it to please themselves rather than others. I learned this from the late Wayne Dyer who followed the teachings of the *Tao Te Ching*. He always encouraged his children to answer their own questions and go within for divine guidance. He understood that children are not ours to own or control but were their own beings with their own minds and paths in life and who were we to stand in their way?

We also see it in various religions where they use control in order to make someone stay within it. The truth is, if something was so great to begin with then no one would need to be forced into anything—they would want to stay. Religion works on a fear basis and they have used fear for many years because it is a quick and easy way to get people to follow them and stay. If you tell an individual or even a child that if they did not stick to certain rules that they would spend eternity in the flames of hell then of course they are not going to want to put a toe out of line. They come out with enormous assumptions and a lot of the time, make stuff up, in order to keep people in the loop. This is why spirituality is winning over religion. Spirituality comes from love. It does not just come from the love of others, it comes from the love of self, the freedom of self. It comes from the freedom to create, to choose, to love who we wish. It also allows us to find this path on our own and create our own opinions. It allows us to seek out and discover. It allows us to remember our greatness and who we truly are, whereas religion tells you what to believe, and what is worse if you do not believe it or if you question anything it is used against you.

If we have ever experienced control then we know its contrasting element—freedom. When we are able to be our true authentic selves then we can live a happy life. We are free to grow, free to attract the wanting, free to create, free to love ourselves. Relationships, friendships, anyone who is in our life should allow us this freedom because they should realise that we are first and foremost freedom seeking creators. We must create for ourselves and love ourselves in order for us to love anyone else. If we have nothing for ourselves, if we have an empty tank, then what do we have for anyone else? We have nothing.

A Journey to Freedom

I was twenty four years old now and unfortunately life was not turning out quite as I expected. I felt completely trapped, lost and unfulfilled. I felt like life was a constant struggle and that I was not going anywhere with it. One evening, I had plans to attend a party for a friend who was going traveling for a few years. I had been unwell all week with a chest infection, which I now realise was a manifestation of life's disappointments but I decided to go as I was always one to honour my commitments and in the end I was glad I did. I sat at the end of the table with another couple I knew and chatted back and forth until the meal was over. From across the table a good friend of mine, the life of the party, arose from her chair and said, 'Okay, now we all have to switch places'. I was placed on the other side of the table facing a woman who seemed to be around my age.

She was very beautiful with a small frame and long dark hair that ran over each collarbone. She seemed perfectly content. She looked across the table at me, a large glass of white wine in one hand and the bottle next to the other and said, 'I hear you are unhappy.' I said nothing for a minute and then I piped up and asked why she had said that. A friend of mine who had been sat at the opposite end of the table to me had told her my story and how I was not enjoying my job anymore and how everything seemed so bleak. I felt at ease with this lady as she seemed to have a good soul. Her next words to me were the words that changed my life forever. 'Have you not read *The Secret*?' She was of course, referring to the first book written by Rhonda Byrne which was sweeping across the world one page at a time. I looked at her with confused eyes. My soul however was not. My soul knew exactly what she was saying even if my mind needed time to catch up. It was one of those moments where everything went in slow motion and settled into itself. It was as if I was in the right place at the right time, like destiny had brought us together for this brief encounter to allow me to evolve. I confessed to her that I had not read it but I felt like I had heard of it. I realise now that my inner being knew exactly what this book was and was waiting for me to line up with the idea of it.

After spending the evening talking back and forth about what she had achieved in her life I felt inspired. Here she was, a single mother of two young children and the world was at her feet. She was already a proud business owner and she still had so much more magic up her sleeve.

Christmas was coming up and I discovered that this book was reasonably priced so I decided to ask one of my sister's for it and she has never let me down. On Christmas Day I opened up the beautifully wrapped present that was sat under my Mum's Christmas tree. I tore open the sparkling red paper and there it was. The book that would start my life. As soon as I got home I was buried in chapter one. Reading every page with care. I could feel my soul floating. It was if I knew this already. It was so simple. I felt like I had been given my life back, my freedom to create the world around me as I wanted it. I wanted to tell everyone, share it with all the people that were around me. I had finally been given a key to freedom and from that moment on I never felt trapped again.

10
Trusting the Universe

When we reach a level of trust, we reach a level of complete alignment with our true selves. We know the power of our creation and we trust that our alignment is so strong that we can always create with ease, no matter what circumstance we are under. We know there is always something wonderful on the way. Having this level of trust enables us to always see the beauty in the world and allows us to flow through life with eagerness. We have gotten rid of the natural habits of creating by default and we know we are always being guided to that end result in what we have put forward to the Universe. It is far more than just trusting in our own abilities, it is trusting in the flow of the Universe. The Universe has a current and we can soon learn to trust that this current will take us to the best places possible. We know that we can push against it and try to force something, but trust knows that we are always better served when we let go and allow ourselves to be swept away.

Trusting the Universe also comes with trusting that our manifestations are positive ones. The more we get to know the Universe and our own power, the more we can begin to expect good things for ourselves. This is something that can take time, but it is a learning curve and the more we create with purpose the more we can expect goodness to come. Expecting comes with knowing and it comes with purpose. The more we live in alignment and know our inner being, the more we know that what we want will come to us without fail. Expecting is a form of gratitude because when we are grateful for the power in which we hold within us and that the Universe holds within itself, we can begin to create that absolute knowing that our desires will come.

Expecting comes with knowing ourselves because when we expect good things to happen, it is because we know who we are and how we purposely create, therefore we expect all that we want to come. Expecting feels good to us and doubt does not. When we doubt we naturally step on what we have desired and therefore never see it. When we doubt we are turning our backs on our inner beings, therefore we cannot see the light through the trees. For some people, depending on where their vibration is, that feeling of doubt is actually a good emotion and they learn to expect doubt. They learn to be okay with doubt. They want something but doubt they will ever have it and so of course, they shall not, but this is only because it feels better to doubt than it does to expect and not receive.

We can only learn to expect the more we use the Universe to create for us, because the more we see it in evidence, the more we expect something to reach us. After we have asked for something we then must expect that it is on its way and it can come to us in many ways. The more aligned we are the faster it will come to us, but the less aligned we are the longer it will take. If something takes a long length of time it creates doubt and instead of seeing that it is the journey that is important, we look for the instant outcome and by doing that we are stopping it from coming. This is all due to balance.

When we tip the scales in more of an expecting way rather than a doubtful way then we are on the right path, but if the slightest bit of doubt starts steering us in the wrong direction it then leads to more asking, but that asking is coming from a place of desperation and therefore it really cannot come. When we hold ourselves in the middle, wanting it but doubting it, we never move forward. If we can all see what a difference it makes when we just put a little more attention on the expecting, we could see the positive path we are on towards that which we desire.

This takes discipline until it becomes natural, because most of us have learned to really go after something and push against it until we get it. Life is not supposed to be that tough. The only reason why one person striving to get somewhere has actually got there is because their gap in that door has widened more at times due to the odd release of energy rather than finding enjoyment of it. When they start struggling again, they close that door and this is why it takes so long for things to reach them. If we can learn to keep that door always open, then the Universe can see through and pass us what we desire. The more we see it evidenced in our lives, the more we expect it to happen and we develop that sense of knowing. It is so important to deliberately focus on what we want and accept that whatever has not yet come is because of us and our energy. You will learn to expect to see little signs and synchronicity that your manifestation is growing and therefore your day will always unfold in just the way you would expect it to.

My Journey to Trust

I remember very clearly the time when I came back to England for a few months after spending time in San Diego with Bobby. I had experienced a strong spiritual awakening. I suddenly knew who I was, what I was and I only wanted to live within that. When I got home I had no money, lots of debt and I had no job. I could not go out and seek a job as I was planning on going back to America soon and besides I did not want to do what I had always been doing. That part of me was suddenly gone and I had to discover who I was once again.

I remember knowing just one thing and that was that I wanted a job that felt good in my heart and that was in the enlightened world that I was now living in. I wanted a job where I could help people, make them feel their own love, guide them to find out who they truly were. I knew it was my destiny. I job hunted for a few days, looking up different types of work but nothing came to me. This kind of job just did not exist and I did not really know where else to look. After those few days, I decided to release it and let the Universe handle it. I knew that the Universe would bring me something and because I did not know what it was or could be it seemed pointless to add frustration into the bowl. Besides, I had held up my end of the deal, I had asked. That was my job and I did it with clarity. The next part of my job was to receive and appreciate which I did a few days later.

At the beginning of my awakening I read books constantly. It was all I did. I just could not get enough. They were all spiritual books or self help books and I read one after another. One book I read changed my life in that moment. I loved that book and read it with great eagerness. In this book, the author told us about her story and about her discoveries. As part of her story, she shared with us what she went through and part of that was her writing. When she first started writing she needed to make money along the way in order to keep her house running as normal as her husband's income was not enough at the time. Her solution was to find work on the same lines as what she was currently doing which was to write. She decided to pick up a handful of magazines and applied to be a writer in the write-in section so she could help those in need using her spiritual gift. Something in her story turned on a light in me and I instantly went to my laptop to find websites and magazines that needed a spiritual writer. The first thing that came to me was a website for freelance writers which I signed up for right away. I could see there were many people out there looking for spiritual writers and I applied for a few despite having little to no experience. I had no work to show apart from the first chapter I wrote for this book, so I decided to send that along with a little about myself. The next day I woke up to a response from a gentleman in Australia. I had applied for a job helping him to develop a book, but he wrote back to inform me that he had in fact found someone already but he wanted to work with me on his website. He wanted a blog done weekly and asked if I could be the one to write it. I was so excited for the opportunity and I jumped on it right away.

From that day I have gone from writing a single weekly blog to writing eight daily blogs for different websites, designing and launching my own website, creating self help videos and ghostwriting four books. This has all been done in the last six months. I trust that the Universe always brings me what I need at the time I need it and not just for myself either, for others. Through my work with others I have come to discover that I learn something just before a client asks me for help, allowing me to guide them to their inner light and find the answer. This has never failed me. Everything happens with perfect timing and because of this entire journey, I have allowed it to come in and leave exactly when it should."

Afterword

In order to appreciate our power in creating we must first appreciate who we are and why we are here. We are born creators. We are creative beings and we are one with the Universe and with each other. We have stepped forth into these physical bodies with extreme enthusiasm to go forth and create a life which is most pleasing to us. When we decided to incarnate here on this earth we knew that we would be creating with the energy that is within us and that all that we create will be a match to that which we are. This life in which we choose shall always change, for without growth there is no change to follow. Therefore, as we are growing, as we are changing, so will our lives and our desires.

To use the Law of Attraction in this world to its greatest advantage we must look within. This law was not just put there for material gain, it was put there to keep the world united, but sadly it has gone the other way. People have learned how powerful it is to put fear onto others to make them follow their rules and do what they believe is right instead of allowing them to form their own opinion. This is because those other opinions hurt them and they do not wish to feel pain, but we all must feel pain because it is where the light is hidden.

If you imagine an ocean and every individual droplet that forms it then this is what we are. We are all droplets in the

Universe, so we are all connected as one. We are not in the ocean, we *are* the ocean. This is the *Law of Divine Oneness.* Our energies all merge together and create within each other and there no longer seems any logical reason to hurt another. In fact, if you are hurting another it is because you are hurting inside. When we feel that negative emotion we cut ourselves off from our inner guidance and we can no longer hear what the Universe is trying to tell us. For those who are wanting to use the Law of Attraction to turn their lives around they must first look in the mirror. We must all come to terms with who we really are and what we represent. We are all love, we are pure positive energy, we are united in our oneness and there is more than enough to go around. No one ever has to go without. In order to help others you do not have to tell them what to do, you do not need to make them read this book or to listen to you, *you must be the example,* because when you shine brightly you give them permission to do the same. The brighter we shine the more they see the divine light and the more they see that light the more they begin to shine themselves. It is time for the awakening and we are all taking part in it so we must step forward into our roles. We must, as individuals, do what it takes to remember who we are and remind others who they truly are and why they are truly here—to stay as one with God through it all.